OUTER SPACE

JOKES

Wacky words compiled by Greg Lee
Daffy drawings made by Robert Court

The Rourke Corporation, Inc.
Vero Beach, Florida 32964

Lee, Greg, 1956-
    Outer space / Wacky words compiled by Greg Lee.
        p. cm. — (The little jokester)
    Summary: Jokes and riddles about outer space. Example: How does Luke Skywalker get from one planet to another? Ewoks.
    ISBN 0-86593-267-0
    1. Outer space—Juvenile humor. 2. Riddles, Juvenile. [1. Outer space—Wit and humor. 2. Jokes. 3. Riddles.] I. Title.
II. Series: Lee, Greg. Little jokester.
PN6231.S645L44 1993
818'.5402—dc20   92-43965
                                                  CIP
                                                     AC

Produced by The Creative Spark
San Clemente, CA.

What did the extraterrestrial say to the slot machine
after it hit the jackpot?
Say, that's a nasty cold you've got there.

Commander: "Why do you whistle all the time on this spaceship?"
Crewman: "It's to keep the aliens away."
Commander: "But there aren't any aliens within a million light
years!"
Crewman: "See how well it works?"

How does an alien count to one hundred?
On its fingers.

"Where are you going with that meal?"
"I want to eat out."

What does an astronaut say when she gets really mad?
"Blast off!"

What kind of music do aliens prefer?
Neptunes.

If Darth Vader misses three pitches, what happens?
The Empire strikes out.

What do aliens drink on the moon?
Craterade.

Two extraterrestrials were standing on a curb when they noticed a traffic light.
One alien turned to the other and said, "Is she winking at you or me?"

Teacher: "Which is lighter, the sun or the earth?"
Student: "The sun."
Teacher: "Why?"
Student: "Because it rises every day."

Space Tourist: "I need a ticket to the moon right away."
Travel Agent: "I'm sorry, madam, but the moon is full."

What do you call an insect who lives in outer space?
Bug Rogers.

What do astronomers and boxers have in common?
They both see stars.

What did the extraterrestrial say when he lost at poker?
E.T. come, E.T. go.

If E.T. phones Saturn, what happens?
It rings.

What kind of fish live in outer space?
Starfish.

How do Venusians shave?
With laser blades.

What's worse than seeing an alien's head in space?
Seeing its tonsils.

What does an alien think of when it sees humans on roller skates?
Meal on wheels.

What do you call an alien space ship that lands inside a volcano? An Unidentified Frying Object.

What do they use to hold together an orbiting space station? Astro knots.

What *does* an alien do when it gets dirty?
It takes a meteor shower.

1st Astronaut: I know this great restaurant on the moon.
2nd Astronaut: *Is the food any good?*
1st Astronaut: Yes, but there's no atmosphere.

What do dentists call an astronaut's cavity?
A black hole.

How does Luke Skywalker get from one planet to another?
Ewoks.

What will they call the next Luke Skywalker movie?
Star Bores.

Shuttle Passenger: "Wow! Our orbit is so high that the people look just like ants."

Shuttle Attendant: "Those are ants. We haven't taken off yet."

Which planet can tell your temperature?
Mercury.

Why is the Milky Way like a Hollywood western?
Because it has shooting stars.

Why are robots so courageous?
They have nerves of steel.

Why do Martians wear white pajamas?
Because their green ones are in the wash.

If the Dog Star is called Sirius, what should scientists call a Cat
    Star?
Curious.

What's green, eats peanuts, and weighs three tons?
A Martian elephant.

How do you make a Neptunian stew?
Make it wait for a long time.

"And they said the TV on Earth was rotten."

Two Martians were hungry after landing on earth, so they promptly
    ate two garbage cans, lid and all.
"What did you think of the cuisine?" asked one.
"The crust was okay, but the filling was kind of rich."

What's another name for a space lamb?
A rocket sheep.

What has 35 legs and goes snap, crackle, pop?
Seven aliens eating Rice Krispies.

At a press conference with the first astronauts back from Jupiter,
    a reporter asked, "What did you see?"
Astronaut: *"We saw evidence of chloropolyzethromethane."*
Reporter: "Would you spell that?"
Astronaut: *"Sure. T-H-A-T."*

What do you do with little green men?
Wait until they ripen.

Why don't chimpanzees live on Mars?
Because there aren't any bananas.

What does the first runner-up receive in the Miss Universe pageant?
A constellation prize.

What kind of years are low in calories?
Light years.

What is the difference between an alien and
peanut butter?
An alien doesn't stick to the roof of your mouth.

Who does Mickey Mouse look for in outer space?
Pluto.